DISHCLOTH
DRESSES

Pick your favorite colors of cotton medium weight yarn
and whip up a darling way to dress up any kitchen!

2

5

8

11

14

17

20

23

26

29

32

36

LEISURE ARTS, INC. • Little Rock, Arkansas

a night on the town

 **EASY**

SHOPPING LIST

Yarn (Medium Weight)
[2.5 ounces, 120 yards
(70 grams, 109 meters) per skein]:
- ☐ Aqua - 37 yards (34 meters)
- ☐ Cream - 3 yards (2.5 meters)

Knitting Needles
Straight needles,
- ☐ Size 7 (4.5 mm)

Additional Supplies
- ☐ Size G (4 mm) crochet hook

TECHNIQUES USED
- M1 *(Figs. 3a & b, page 42)*
- K2 tog *(Fig. 4, page 43)*
- K3 tog *(Fig. 9, page 45)*
- Slip 1 as if to **knit**, K2 tog, PSSO
  (Fig. 10, page 45)
- Changing Colors *(page 45)*
- Basic Crochet Stitches *(page 46)*

INSTRUCTIONS
SKIRT
With Aqua, cast on 37 sts.

Row 1: Knit across.

Row 2 (Right side)**:** Knit across.

Row 3: K2, P 33, K2.

Row 4: K5, P3, (K3, P3) 4 times, K5.

Row 5: K2, P3, (K3, P3) 5 times, K2.

Row 6: K5, P3, (K3, P3) 4 times, K5.

Row 7: K2, P 33, K2.

Row 8: Knit across.

Row 9: K2, P 33, K2.

Row 10: K2, P3, (K3, P3) 5 times, K2.

Row 11: K5, P3, (K3, P3) 4 times, K5.

Row 12: K2, P3, (K3, P3) 5 times, K2.

Row 13: K2, P 33, K2.

Row 14: Knit across.

Row 15: K2, P 33, K2.

Rows 16-21: Repeat Rows 14 and 15, 3 times.

Rows 22-27: Repeat Rows 10-15; at end of Row 27, cut Aqua.

WAIST
Row 1: With Cream, K2, (slip 1, K2 tog, PSSO) 5 times, K3, K3 tog 5 times, K2: 17 sts.

Row 2: K2 tog 4 times, K1, K2 tog 4 times: 9 sts.

Rows 3-6: Knit across; at end of Row 6, cut Cream.

BODICE
Row 1: With Aqua, K3, (M1, K3) twice: 11 sts.

Row 2: K1, P9, K1.

Row 3: K3, M1, K5, M1, K3: 13 sts.

Row 4: K1, P 11, K1.

Row 5: Knit across.

Row 6: K1, P 11, K1.

NECK SHAPING
K4, bind off next 5 sts in **knit**, knit across: 4 sts **each** side.

First Side - Row 1: K1, P3, leave remaining 4 sts unworked for Second Side; **turn**.

Row 2: K4.

Row 3: K1, P3.

Bind off all sts on First Side in **knit**.

Second Side - Row 1: With **wrong** side facing and Aqua, P3, K1.

Row 2: K4.

Row 3: P3, K1.

Bind off 3 sts in **knit**; do **not** cut yarn one st.

Slip st onto crochet hook, ch 12; with **right** side facing, join with slip st to first st on First Side; slip st evenly around entire neckline including each ch; finish off.

princess for a day

 EASY

Shown on page 7.

SHOPPING LIST

Yarn (Medium Weight)
[3 ounces, 150 yards
(85 grams, 138 meters) per skein]:
☐ 55 yards (50.5 meters)

Knitting Needles
Straight needles,
☐ Size 7 (4.5 mm)

Additional Supplies
☐ Size G (4 mm) crochet hook

TECHNIQUES USED
M1 *(Figs. 3a & b, page 42)*
K2 tog *(Fig. 4, page 43)*
SSK *(Figs. 7a-c, page 44)*
Slip 1 as if to **knit**, K1, PSSO
    (Figs. 8a & b, page 44)
Slip 1 as if to **knit**, K2 tog, PSSO
    (Fig. 10, page 45)
Basic Crochet Stitches *(page 46)*

INSTRUCTIONS
Wind approximately 3 yards
(2.5 meters) of yarn into a separate
ball to use for Neck Shaping.

SKIRT
Cast on 44 sts.

Row 1 (Right side)**:** K4, (slip 1 as if to
purl, K4) across.

Row 2: K4, (P1, K4) across.

Repeat Rows 1 and 2 for pattern until
Skirt measures approximately 5"
(12.5 cm) from cast on edge, ending
by working Row 2.

WAIST & BODICE
Row 1: K1, (SSK, K1, slip 1 as if to
purl, K1) 4 times, K2 tog, K1, (slip 1
as if to **purl**, K1, K2 tog, K1) across:
35 sts.

Row 2: (K1, K2 tog, P1) across to last
3 sts, K2 tog, K1: 26 sts.

Row 3: K1, ★ slip 1 as if to **knit**, K2 tog, PSSO; repeat from ★ across to last st, K1: 10 sts.

Row 4: K1, P8, K1.

Row 5: Knit across.

Row 6: K1, P8, K1.

Row 7: K3, M1, K4, M1, K3: 12 sts.

Row 8: K1, P 10, K1.

Row 9: Knit across.

Rows 10-12: Repeat Rows 8 and 9 once, then repeat Row 8 once **more**.

NECK SHAPING

Both sides of Neck are worked at the same time, using separate yarn for **each** side.

Row 1: K4, K2 tog; with second yarn, SSK, K4: 5 sts **each** side.

Row 2: K1, P3, slip 1 as if to **purl**; with second yarn, slip 1 as if to **purl**, P3, K1.

Row 3: K3, K2 tog; with second yarn, SSK, K3: 4 sts **each** side.

Row 4: K1, P2, slip 1 as if to **purl**; with second yarn, slip 1 as if to **purl**, P2, K1.

Row 5: K2, K2 tog; with second yarn, SSK, K2: 3 sts **each** side.

Row 6: K1, P1, slip 1 as if to **purl**; with second yarn, slip 1 as if to **purl**, P1, K1.

Row 7: K1, K2 tog; with second yarn, SSK, K1: 2 sts **each** side.

Row 8: K1, P1; with second yarn, P1, K1.

Row 9: Slip 1 as if to **knit**, K1, PSSO, do **not** cut yarn; with second yarn, slip 1 as if to **knit**, K1, PSSO, cut yarn and draw through st: one st.

Slip st onto crochet hook, ch 12; with **right** side facing, join with slip st to first st on second side; finish off.

company's coming

SHOPPING LIST

Yarn (Medium Weight)
[2 ounces, 95 yards
(56 grams, 86 meters) per skein]:
☐ Variegated - 20 yards
     (18.5 meters)
[2.5 ounces, 120 yards
(70 grams, 109 meters) per skein]:
☐ Green - 16 yards (14.5 meters)

Knitting Needles
Straight needles,
☐ Size 7 (4.5 mm)

Additional Supplies
☐ Size G (4 mm) crochet hook

TECHNIQUES USED
• M1 *(Figs. 3a & b, page 42)*
• K2 tog *(Fig. 4, page 43)*
• P2 tog *(Fig. 5, page 43)*
• SSK *(Figs. 7a-c, page 44)*
• Changing Colors *(page 45)*
• Basic Crochet Stitches *(page 46)*

INSTRUCTIONS
SKIRT
With Green, cast on 30 sts.

Row 1: Knit across; do **not** cut Green unless specified.

Row 2 (Right side)**:** With Variegated, knit across.

Row 3: K2, P 26, K2; do **not** cut Variegated unless specified.

Rows 4 and 5: With Green, knit across.

Rows 6-27: Repeat Rows 2-5, 5 times; then repeat Rows 2 and 3 once **more**.

WAIST & BODICE

Row 1: With Green, K3, SSK 6 times, K2 tog 6 times, K3: 18 sts.

Row 2: Knit across.

Row 3: With Variegated, K2, SSK 3 times, K2, K2 tog 3 times, K2: 12 sts.

Row 4: K1, P2 tog twice, P2, P2 tog twice, K1: 8 sts.

Row 5: With Green, K2, M1, K4, M1, K2: 10 sts.

Row 6: Knit across.

Row 7: With Variegated, K2, M1, K6, M1, K2: 12 sts.

Row 8: K2, P8, K2.

Rows 9 and 10: With Green, knit across; at end of Row 10, cut Green.

Row 11: With Variegated, knit across.

Row 12: K2, P8, K2.

Rows 13-16: Repeat Rows 11 and 12 twice.

NECK SHAPING

K3, bind off next 6 sts in **knit**, knit across: 3 sts **each** side.

First Side - Row 1: K3, leave remaining 3 sts unworked for Second Side; **turn.**

Rows 2-8: K3.

Bind off all sts on First Side in **knit.**

Second Side - Row 1: With **wrong** side facing and Variegated, K3.

Rows 2-8: K3.

Bind off 2 sts in **knit**; do **not** cut yarn: one st.

Slip st onto crochet hook, ch 12; with **right** side facing, join with slip st to first st on First Side; finish off.

dress with apron

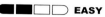 **EASY**

SHOPPING LIST

Yarn (Medium Weight)

[2.5 ounces, 120 yards
(70 grams, 109 meters) per skein]:
☐ Yellow - 27 yards (24.5 meters)
[2 ounces, 95 yards
(56 grams, 86 meters) per skein]:
☐ Variegated - 13 yards
   (12 meters)

Knitting Needles

Straight needles,
☐ Size 7 (4.5 mm)

Additional Supplies

☐ Size G (4 mm) crochet hook

TECHNIQUES USED

M1 *(Figs. 3a & b, page 42)*
K2 tog *(Fig. 4, page 43)*
P2 tog *(Fig. 5, page 43)*
SSK *(Figs. 7a-c, page 44)*
Changing Colors *(Fig. 11, page 45)*
Basic Crochet Stitches *(page 46)*

INSTRUCTIONS

SKIRT

Wind approximately 5 yards
(4.5 meters) of Yellow into a separate
ball to use beginning with Row 12.

With Yellow, cast on 37 sts.

Row 1: K1, (P1, K1) across.

Row 2 (Right side)**:** Knit across.

Rows 3-11: Repeat Rows 1 and 2, 4
times; then repeat Row 1 once **more**.

Row 12: K8, drop Yellow; with
Variegated, K 21, drop Variegated;
with second Yellow, K8.

Row 13: (K1, P1) 4 times; with
Variegated, K 21; with Yellow, (P1,
K1) 4 times.

Row 14: K8; with Variegated, K 21;
with Yellow, K8.

Row 15: (K1, P1) 4 times; with
Variegated, P 21; (P1, K1) 4 times.

Repeat Rows 14 and 15 for pattern, until Skirt measures approximately 4½" (11.5 cm) from cast on edge, ending by working Row 15.

WAIST & BODICE

Row 1: SSK 4 times; with Variegated, SSK 5 times, K1, K2 tog 5 times; with Yellow, K2 tog 4 times: 19 sts.

Row 2: P2 tog twice; with Variegated, P2 tog twice, P3, P2 tog twice; with Yellow, P2 tog twice: 11 sts.

Row 3: K2; with Variegated, SSK, K3, K2 tog; with Yellow, K2: 9 sts.

Row 4: K1, P1; with Variegated, P5; with Yellow, P1, K1.

Row 5: K2; with Variegated, K1, M1, K3, M1, K1; with Yellow, K2: 11 sts.

Row 6: K1, P1; with Variegated, P7; with Yellow, P1, K1.

Row 7: K2; with Variegated, K1, M1, K5, M1, K1; with Yellow, K2: 13 sts.

Row 8: K1, P1; with Variegated, P9; with Yellow, P1, K1.

Row 9: K2; with Variegated, P9; with Yellow, K2.

Row 10: K1, P1, cut Yellow; with Variegated, P9, cut Variegated; with Yellow, P1, K1.

Row 11: With Yellow, knit across.

Row 12: K1, P 11, K1.

NECK SHAPING

K4, bind off next 5 sts in **knit**, knit across: 4 sts **each** side.

First Side - Row 1: K1, P3, leave remaining 4 sts unworked for Second Side; **turn**.

Row 2: K4.

Row 3: K1, P3.

Bind off all sts on First Side in **knit**.

Second Side - Row 1: With **wrong** side facing and Yellow, P3, K1.

Row 2: K4.

Row 3: P3, K1.

Bind off 3 sts in **knit**; do **not** cut yarn one st.

Slip st onto crochet hook, ch 12; with **right** side facing, join with slip st to first st on First Side; slip st evenly around entire neckline including each ch; finish off.

going dancing #1

 **EASY**

SHOPPING LIST

Yarn (Medium Weight) MEDIUM 4

[2.5 ounces, 120 yards
(70 grams, 109 meters) per skein]:
- ☐ Blue - 20 yards (18.5 meters)
- ☐ Ecru - 20 yards (18.5 meters)

Knitting Needles

Straight needles,
- ☐ Size 7 (4.5 mm)

Additional Supplies

- ☐ Size G (4 mm) crochet hook

TECHNIQUES USED

- YO *(Fig. 2, page 42)*
- M1 *(Figs. 3a & b, page 42)*
- P2 tog *(Fig. 5, page 43)*
- K2 tog tbl *(Fig. 6, page 43)*
- Changing Colors *(page 45)*
- Basic Crochet Stitches *(page 46)*

INSTRUCTIONS
SKIRT

With Blue, cast on 40 sts.

Row 1: K2, P 36, K2; do **not** cut Blue unless specified.

Row 2 (Right side)**:** With Ecru, knit across.

Row 3: K2, P 36, K2; do **not** cut Ecru unless specified.

Row 4: With Blue, K2, K2 tog tbl twice, (YO, K1) 4 times, ★ K2 tog tbl 4 times, (YO, K1) 4 times; repeat from ★ once **more**, K2 tog tbl twice, K2.

Row 5: Knit across.

Rows 6-25: Repeat Rows 2-5, 5 times; at end of Row 25, cut Blue.

WAIST & BODICE

Row 1: With Ecru, K1, K2 tog tbl across to last st, K1: 21 sts.

Row 2: K1, P2 tog 4 times, P3, P2 tog 4 times, K1: 13 sts.

Row 3: K1, (K2 tog tbl, K1) across: 9 sts.

Row 4: K1, P7, K1.

Row 5: Knit across.

Row 6: K1, P7, K1.

Row 7: K3, (M1, K3) twice: 11 sts.

Row 8: K1, P9, K1.

Row 9: K3, M1, K5, M1, K3: 13 sts.

Row 10: K1, P 11, K1.

Row 11: Knit across.

Row 12: K1, P 11, K1.

NECK SHAPING

K4, bind off next 5 sts in **knit**, knit across: 4 sts **each** side.

First Side - Row 1: K1, P3, leave remaining 4 sts unworked for Second Side; **turn.**

Row 2: K4.

Row 3: K1, P3.

Bind off all sts on First Side in **knit**.

Second Side - Row 1: With **wrong** side facing and Ecru, P3, K1.

Row 2: K4.

Row 3: P3, K1.

Bind off 3 sts in **knit**; do **not** cut yarn: one st.

Slip st onto crochet hook, ch 12; with **right** side facing, join with slip st to first st on First Side; slip st evenly around entire neckline including each ch; finish off.

going dancing #2

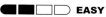 **EASY**

Shown on page 19.

SHOPPING LIST

Yarn (Medium Weight)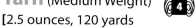
[2.5 ounces, 120 yards
(70 grams, 109 meters) per skein]:
- ☐ White - 23 yards (21 meters)
- ☐ Aqua - 5 yards (4.5 meters)
- ☐ Peach - 5 yards (4.5 meters)
- ☐ Yellow - 5 yards (4.5 meters)

Knitting Needles
Straight needles,
- ☐ Size 7 (4.5 mm)

Additional Supplies
- ☐ Size G (4 mm) crochet hook

TECHNIQUES USED

- YO *(Fig. 2, page 42)*
- M1 *(Figs. 3a & b, page 42)*
- P2 tog *(Fig. 5, page 43)*
- K2 tog tbl *(Fig. 6, page 43)*
- Changing Colors *(page 45)*
- Basic Crochet Stitches *(page 46)*

INSTRUCTIONS

SKIRT
With White, cast on 40 sts.

Row 1: K2, P 36, K2; do **not** cut White unless specified.

Row 2 (Right side)**:** With Aqua, knit across.

Row 3: K2, P 36, K2; cut yarn.

Row 4: With White, K2,
K2 tog tbl twice, (YO, K1) 4 times,
★ K2 tog tbl 4 times, (YO, K1) 4
times; repeat from ★ once **more**,
K2 tog tbl twice, K2.

Row 5: Knit across.

Rows 6 and 7: With Peach, repeat Rows 2 and 3.

Rows 8 and 9: Repeat Rows 4 and 5.

Rows 10 and 11: With Yellow, repeat Rows 2 and 3.

Rows 12 and 13: Repeat Rows 4 and 5.

Rows 14-23: Repeat Rows 2-11.

WAIST & BODICE

Row 1: With White, K1, K2 tog tbl across to last st, K1: 21 sts.

Row 2: K1, P2 tog 4 times, P3, P2 tog 4 times, K1: 13 sts.

Row 3: K1, (K2 tog tbl, K1) across: 9 sts.

Row 4: K1, P7, K1.

Row 5: Knit across.

Row 6: K1, P7, K1.

Row 7: K3, (M1, K3) twice: 11 sts.

Row 8: K1, P9, K1.

Row 9: K3, M1, K5, M1, K3: 13 sts.

Row 10: K1, P 11, K1.

Row 11: Knit across.

Row 12: K1, P 11, K1.

NECK SHAPING

K4, bind off next 5 sts in **knit**, knit across: 4 sts **each** side.

First Side - Row 1: K1, P3, leave remaining 4 sts unworked for Second Side; **turn.**

Row 2: K4.

Row 3: K1, P3.

Bind off all sts on First Side in **knit**.

Second Side - Row 1: With **wrong** side facing and White, P3, K1.

Row 2: K4.

Row 3: P3, K1.

Bind off 3 sts in **knit**; do **not** cut yarn: one st.

Slip st onto crochet hook, ch 12; with **right** side facing, join with slip st to first st on First Side; slip st evenly around entire neckline including each ch; finish off.

wedding day

 **EASY**

TECHNIQUES USED
• YO *(Fig. 2, page 42)*
• M1 *(Figs. 3a & b, page 42)*
• K2 tog *(Fig. 4, page 43)*
• P2 tog *(Fig. 5, page 43)*
• SSK *(Figs. 7a-c, page 44)*
• Basic Crochet Stitches *(page 46)*

INSTRUCTIONS
SKIRT
Cast on 35 sts.

Rows 1 and 2: Knit across.

Row 3: K3, P 29, K3.

Row 4 (Right side)**:** Knit across.

Row 5: K3, P 29, K3.

Rows 6 and 7: Knit across.

Row 8: K3, (K2 tog, YO) across to last 4 sts, K4.

Rows 9 and 10: Knit across.

Row 11: K3, P 29, K3.

Rows 12 and 13: Knit across.

Row 14: K3, (K2 tog, YO) across to last 4 sts, K4.

Rows 15 and 16: Knit across.

Row 17: K3, P 29, K3.

Rows 18-25: Repeat Rows 16 and 17, 4 times.

WAIST & BODICE

Row 1: K1, SSK 8 times, K1, K2 tog 8 times, K1: 19 sts.

Row 2: K1, P2 tog 4 times, P1, P2 tog 4 times, K1: 11 sts.

Row 3: K2, SSK, K3, K2 tog, K2: 9 sts.

Row 4: K1, P7, K1.

Row 5: Knit across.

Row 6: K1, P7, K1.

Row 7: K3, (M1, K3) twice: 11 sts.

Row 8: K1, P9, K1.

Row 9: K3, M1, K5, M1, K3: 13 sts.

Row 10: K1, P 11, K1.

Row 11: Knit across.

Row 12: K1, P 11, K1.

NECK SHAPING

K4, bind off next 5 sts in **knit**, knit across: 4 sts **each** side.

First Side - Row 1: K1, P3, leave remaining 4 sts unworked for Second Side; **turn**.

Row 2: K4.

Row 3: K1, P3.

Bind off all sts on First Side in **knit**.

Second Side - Row 1: With **wrong** side facing, P3, K1.

Row 2: K4.

Row 3: P3, K1.

Bind off 3 sts in **knit**; do **not** cut yarn: one st.

Slip st onto crochet hook, ch 12; with **right** side facing, join with slip st to first st on First Side; slip st evenly around entire neckline including each ch; finish off.

happy day #1

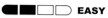

Shown on page 25.

SHOPPING LIST

Yarn (Medium Weight)
[2.5 ounces, 120 yards
(70 grams, 109 meters) per skein]:
- ☐ Cream - 26 yards (24 meters)
- ☐ Aqua - 11 yards (10 meters)
- ☐ Peach - 3 yards (2.5 meters)

Knitting Needles
Straight needles,
- ☐ Size 7 (4.5 mm)

Additional Supplies
- ☐ Size G (4 mm) crochet hook

TECHNIQUES USED

- M1 *(Figs. 3a & b, page 42)*
- K2 tog *(Fig. 4, page 43)*
- P2 tog *(Fig. 5, page 43)*
- SSK *(Figs. 7a-c, page 44)*
- Changing Colors *(page 45)*
- Basic Crochet Stitches *(page 46)*

INSTRUCTIONS
SKIRT
With Aqua, cast on 35 sts.

Row 1: Knit across; cut Aqua.

Row 2 (Right side)**:** With Cream, knit across.

Row 3: K3, P 29, K3.

Rows 4 and 5: Repeat Rows 2 and 3; at end of Row 5, cut Cream.

Rows 6 and 7: With Aqua, knit across; do **not** cut Aqua.

Row 8: With Peach, knit across.

Row 9: K3, P 29, K3; cut Peach.

Rows 10 and 11: With Aqua, knit across; at end of Row 11, cut Aqua.

Row 12: With Cream, knit across.

Row 13: K3, P 29, K3.

Repeat Rows 12 and 13 for pattern, until Skirt measures approximately 4¾" (12 cm) from cast on edge, ending by working Row 13.

WAIST & BODICE

Row 1: K1, SSK 8 times, K1, K2 tog 8 times, K1: 19 sts.

Row 2: K1, P2 tog 4 times, P1, P2 tog 4 times, K1: 11 sts.

Row 3: Knit across.

Row 4: K1, P9, K1.

Row 5: K3, M1, K5, M1, K3: 13 sts.

Row 6: K1, P 11, P1.

Row 7: K3, M1, K7, M1, K3: 15 sts.

Row 8: K1, P 13, K1.

Row 9: Knit across.

Row 10: K1, P 13, K1.

Rows 11 and 12: With Peach, knit across; at end of Row 12, cut Peach.

Row 13: With Cream, knit across.

Row 14: K1, P 13, K1; cut Cream.

NECK SHAPING

With Aqua, K5, bind off next 5 sts in **knit**, knit across: 5 sts **each** side.

First Side - Row 1: K5, leave remaining 5 sts unworked for Second Side; **turn**.

Rows 2-6: K5.

Bind off all sts on First Side in **knit**.

Second Side - Row 1: With **wrong** side facing and Aqua, K5.

Rows 2-6: K5.

Bind off 4 sts in **knit**; do **not** cut yarn: one st.

Slip st onto crochet hook, ch 12; with **right** side facing, join with slip st to first st on First Side; finish off.

happy day #2

 **EASY**

SHOPPING LIST

Yarn (Medium Weight)
[2 ounces, 95 yards
(56 grams, 86 meters) per skein]:
- ☐ Variegated - 28 yards
  (25.5 meters)
[2.5 ounces, 120 yards
(70 grams, 109 meters) per skein]:
- ☐ Yellow - 12 yards (11 meters)

Knitting Needles
Straight needles,
- ☐ Size 7 (4.5 mm)

Additional Supplies
- ☐ Size G (4 mm) crochet hook
- ☐ Safety pin

TECHNIQUES USED
- M1 *(Figs. 3a & b, page 42)*
- K2 tog *(Fig. 4, page 43)*
- P2 tog *(Fig. 5, page 43)*
- SSK *(Figs. 7a-c, page 44)*
- Changing Colors *(page 45)*
- Basic Crochet Stitches *(page 46)*

INSTRUCTIONS
SKIRT
With Yellow, cast on 35 sts.

Row 1: Knit across; cut Yellow.

Row 2 (Right side)**:** With Variegated, knit across.

Row 3: K3, P 29, K3.

Rows 4 and 5: Repeat Rows 2 and 3; at end of Row 5, do **not** cut Variegated.

Rows 6 and 7: With Yellow, knit across; at end of Row 7, do **not** cut Yellow.

Row 8: With Variegated, knit across.

Row 9: K3, P 29, K3; do **not** cut Variegated.

Rows 10 and 11: With Yellow, knit across; at end of Row 11, cut Yellow.

Row 12: With Variegated, knit across.

Row 13: K3, P 29, K3.

Repeat Rows 12 and 13 for pattern, until Skirt measures approximately 4¾" (12 cm) from cast on edge, ending by working Row 13.

WAIST & BODICE

Row 1: K1, SSK 8 times, K1, K2 tog 8 times, K1: 19 sts.

Row 2: K1, P2 tog 4 times, P1, P2 tog 4 times, K1: 11 sts.

Row 3: Knit across.

Row 4: K1, P9, K1.

Row 5: K3, M1, K5, M1, K3: 13 sts.

Row 6: K1, P 11, P1.

Row 7: K3, M1, K7, M1, K3: 15 sts.

Row 8: K1, P 13, K1.

Row 9: Knit across.

Row 10: K1, P 13, K1; do **not** cut Variegated.

Rows 11 and 12: With Yellow, knit across; at end of Row 12, do **not** cut Yellow.

Row 13: With Variegated, knit across.

Row 14: K1, P 13, K1; cut Variegated.

NECK SHAPING

With Yellow, K5, bind off next 5 sts in **knit**, knit across: 5 sts **each** side.

First Side - Row 1: K5, leave remaining 5 sts unworked for Second Side; **turn.**

Rows 2-6: K5.

Bind off all sts on First Side in **knit**.

Second Side - Row 1: With **wrong** side facing and Yellow, K5.

Rows 2-6: K5.

Bind off 4 sts in **knit**; do **not** cut yarn: one st.

Slip st onto crochet hook, ch 12; with **right** side facing, join with slip st to first st on First Side; finish off.

prom date #1

Shown on page 31.

SHOPPING LIST

Yarn (Medium Weight)
[2.5 ounces, 120 yards
(70 grams, 109 meters) per skein]:
☐ Lavender - 26 yards
(24 meters)
[2 ounces, 95 yards
(56 grams, 86 meters) per skein]:
☐ Variegated - 10 yards
(9 meters)

Knitting Needles
Straight needles,
☐ Size 7 (4.5 mm)

Additional Supplies
☐ Size G (4 mm) crochet hook

TECHNIQUES USED
M1 *(Figs. 3a & b, page 42)*
K2 tog *(Fig. 4, page 43)*
P2 tog *(Fig. 5, page 43)*
SSK *(Figs. 7a-c, page 44)*
Changing Colors *(Fig. 11, page 45)*
Basic Crochet Stitches *(page 46)*

INSTRUCTIONS
SKIRT
Wind approximately 11 yards
(10 meters) of Lavender into a
separate ball to use beginning with
Row 2.

With Lavender, cast on 35 sts.

Row 1: Knit across.

Row 2 (Right side)**:** K 11, drop
Lavender; with Variegated, K 13, drop
Variegated; with second Lavender,
K 11.

Row 3: K 11; with Variegated, P 13;
with Lavender, K 11.

Rows 4-19: Repeat Rows 2 and 3, 8
times.

Row 20: K 11; with Variegated, SSK,
K9, K2 tog; with Lavender, K 11: 33 sts.

Row 21: K 11; with Variegated, P 11;
with Lavender, K 11.

Row 22: K 11; with Variegated, SSK,
K7, K2 tog; with Lavender, K 11: 31 sts.

Row 23: K 11; with Variegated, P9; with Lavender, K 11.

Row 24: K 11; with Variegated, SSK, K5, K2 tog; with Lavender, K 11: 29 sts.

Row 25: K 11; with Variegated, P7; with Lavender, K 11.

Row 26: K 11; with Variegated, SSK, K3, K2 tog; with Lavender, K 11: 27 sts.

Row 27: K 11; with Variegated, P5; with Lavender, K 11.

Row 28: K8, SSK, K1; with Variegated, K5; with Lavender, K1, K2 tog, K8: 25 sts.

Row 29: K 10; with Variegated, P5; with Lavender, K 10.

Row 30: K1, SSK, K7; with Variegated, K5; with Lavender, K7, K2 tog, K1: 23 sts.

Row 31: K9, cut Lavender; with Variegated, P5, cut Variegated; with Lavender, K9.

WAIST & BODICE

Row 1: K1, SSK 5 times, K1, K2 tog 5 times, K1: 13 sts.

Row 2: K1, K2 tog twice, K3, K2 tog twice, K1: 9 sts.

Rows 3 and 4: Knit across.

Row 5: K3, (M1, K3) twice: 11 sts.

Row 6: Knit across.

Row 7: K3, M1, K5, M1, K3: 13 sts.

Rows 8-10: Knit across.

NECK SHAPING
K4, bind off next 5 sts in **knit**, knit across: 4 sts **each** side.

First Side - Row 1: K4, leave remaining 4 sts unworked for Second Side; **turn**.

Rows 2-4: K4.

Bind off all sts on First Side in **knit**.

Second Side - Row 1: With **wrong** side facing and Lavender, K4.

Rows 2-4: K4.

Bind off 3 sts in **knit**; do **not** cut yarn one st.

Slip st onto crochet hook, ch 12; with **right** side facing, join with slip st to first st on First Side; slip st evenly around entire neckline including each ch; finish off.

prom date #2

 **EASY**

SHOPPING LIST

Yarn (Medium Weight)
[2.5 ounces, 120 yards
(70 grams, 109 meters) per skein]:
☐ Pink - 25 yards (23 meters)
[2 ounces, 95 yards
(56 grams, 86 meters) per skein]:
☐ Variegated - 15 yards
(13.5 meters)

Knitting Needles
Straight needles,
☐ Size 7 (4.5 mm)

Additional Supplies
☐ Size G (4 mm) crochet hook

TECHNIQUES USED
• M1 *(Figs. 3a & b, page 42)*
• K2 tog *(Fig. 4, page 43)*
• P2 tog *(Fig. 5, page 43)*
• SSK *(Figs. 7a-c, page 44)*
• Changing Colors *(Fig. 11, page 45)*
• Basic Crochet Stitches *(page 46)*

INSTRUCTIONS
SKIRT
Wind approximately 11 yards
(10 meters) of Pink into a separate
ball to use beginning with Row 2.

With Pink, cast on 35 sts.

Row 1: K1, (P1, K1) across.

Row 2 (Right side)**:** K1, (P1, K1) 5
times, drop Pink; with Variegated,
K 13, drop Variegated; with second
Pink, K1, (P1, K1) 5 times.

Row 3: K1, (P1, K1) 5 times; with
Variegated, P 13; with Pink, K1, (P1,
K1) 5 times.

Rows 4-19: Repeat Rows 2 and 3, 8
times.

Row 20: K1, (P1, K1) 5 times; with
Variegated, SSK, K9, K2 tog; with
Pink, K1, (P1, K1) 5 times: 33 sts.

Row 21: K1, (P1, K1) 5 times; with Variegated, P 11; with Pink, K1, (P1, K1) 5 times.

Row 22: K1, (P1, K1) 5 times; with Variegated, SSK, K7, K2 tog; with Pink, K1, (P1, K1) 5 times: 31 sts.

Row 23: K1, (P1, K1) 5 times; with Variegated, P9; with Pink, K1, (P1, K1) 5 times.

Row 24: K1, (P1, K1) 5 times; with Variegated, SSK, K5, K2 tog; with Pink, K1, (P1, K1) 5 times: 29 sts.

Row 25: K1, (P1, K1) 5 times; with Variegated, P7; with Pink, K1, (P1, K1) 5 times.

Row 26: K1, (P1, K1) 5 times; with Variegated, SSK, K3, K2 tog; with Pink, K1, (P1, K1) 5 times: 27 sts.

Row 27: K1, (P1, K1) 5 times; with Variegated, P5; with Pink, K1, (P1, K1) 5 times.

Row 28: (K1, P1) 4 times, SSK, K1; with Variegated, K5; with Pink, K1, K2 tog, (P1, K1) 4 times: 25 sts.

Row 29: (K1, P1) 5 times; with Variegated, P5; with Pink, (P1, K1) 5 times.

Row 30: K1, SSK, P1, (K1, P1) 3 times with Variegated, K5; with Pink, P1, (K1, P1) 3 times, K2 tog, K1: 23 sts.

Row 31: K2, P1, (K1, P1) 3 times, cut Pink; with Variegated, P5, cut Variegated; with Pink, P1, (K1, P1) 3 times, K2.

WAIST & BODICE

Row 1: K1, SSK 5 times, K1, K2 tog 5 times, K1: 13 sts.

Row 2: K1, P2 tog twice, P3, P2 tog twice, K1, cut Pink: 9 sts.

Row 3: With Variegated, knit across.

Row 4: K1, P7, K1.

Row 5: K3, (M1, K3) twice: 11 sts.

Row 6: K1, P9, K1.

Row 7: K3, M1, K5, M1, K3: 13 sts.

Row 8: K1, P 11, K1.

Row 9: Knit across.

Row 10: K1, P 11, K1.

NECK SHAPING

K4, bind off next 5 sts in **knit**, knit across: 4 sts **each** side.

First Side - Row 1: K1, P3, leave remaining 4 sts unworked for Second Side unworked; **turn.**

Row 2: K4.

Row 3: K1, P3.

Bind off all sts on First Side in **knit.**

Second Side - Row 1: With **wrong** side facing and Variegated, P3, K1.

Row 2: K4.

Row 3: P3, K1.

Bind off 3 sts in **knit**; do **not** cut yarn: one st.

Slip st onto crochet hook, ch 12; with **right** side facing, slip st in first st on First Side; slip st evenly around entire neckline including each ch; finish off.

garden party

■■□▷ **EASY**

SHOPPING LIST

Yarn (Medium Weight)
[2.5 ounces, 120 yards
(70 grams, 109 meters) per skein]:
☐ 47 yards (43 meters)

Knitting Needles

Straight needles,
☐ Size 7 (4.5 mm)

Additional Supplies

☐ Size G (4 mm) crochet hook

TECHNIQUES USED

• Knit increase *(Figs. 1a & b, page 41)*
• M1 *(Figs. 3a & b, page 42)*
• K2 tog *(Fig. 4, page 43)*
• SSK *(Figs. 7a-c, page 44)*
• K3 tog *(Fig. 9, page 45)*
• Slip 1 as if to **knit**, K2 tog, PSSO
  (Fig. 10, page 45)
• Basic Crochet Stitches *(page 46)*

INSTRUCTIONS

Wind approximately 3 yards
(2.5 meters) of yarn into a separate
ball to use for Neck Shaping.

SKIRT

FIRST POINT
Cast on 2 sts.

Row 1: Work knit increase, K1: 3 sts.

Rows 2-5: Work knit increase, knit
across: 7 sts.

Cut yarn; slide sts to secure end of
needle.

NEXT 3 POINTS
Cast 2 sts onto empty needle.

Row 1: With needle containing
previous point(s), work knit increase
K1: 3 sts (previous points are not
considered in st count).

Rows 2-5: Work knit increase, knit across: 7 sts.

Cut yarn; slide sts to same end of needle as previous point(s).

FIFTH POINT
Cast 2 sts onto empty needle.

Row 1: With needle containing previous points, work knit increase, K1: 3 sts (previous points are not considered in st count).

Rows 2-5: Work knit increase, knit across: 7 sts.

Do **not** cut yarn; you will have a total of 35 sts on needle.

BODY
Row 1 (Right side)**:** Knit across.

Row 2: (K6, work knit increase) 4 times, K7: 39 sts.

Row 3: K7, (slip 1 as if to **purl**, K7) across.

Row 4: K7, (P1, K7) across.

Repeat Rows 3 and 4 for pattern until Skirt measures approximately 5" (12.5 cm) from tip of center point, ending by working Row 4.

WAIST & BODICE
Row 1: K1, (K2 tog, K1) twice, ★ slip 1 as if to **purl**, K1, (K2 tog, K1) twice: repeat from ★ across: 29 sts.

Row 2: K1, K2 tog twice, P1, ★ K2 tog, K1, K2 tog, P1; repeat from ★ 2 times **more**, K2 tog twice, K1: 19 sts.

Row 3: ★ Slip 1, K2 tog, PSSO, K1; repeat from ★ 3 times **more**, K3 tog: 9 sts.

Rows 4-6: Knit across.

Row 7: K3, (M1, K3) twice: 11 sts.

Row 8: Knit across.

Row 9: K3, M1, K5, M1, K3: 13 sts.

Rows 10-14: Knit across.

NECK SHAPING
Both sides of Neck are worked at the same time, using separate yarn for each side.

Row 1: K5, K2 tog; with second yarn, K6: 6 sts **each** side.

Row 2: Knit across; with second yarn, knit across.

Row 3: K4, K2 tog; with second yarn, SSK, K4: 5 sts **each** side.

Row 4: K5; with second yarn, K5.

Row 5: K3, K2 tog; with second yarn, SSK, K3: 4 sts **each** side.

Row 6: K4; with second yarn, K4.

Row 7: K2, K2 tog; with second yarn, SSK, K2: 3 sts **each** side.

Row 8: K3; with second yarn, K3.

Row 9: Slip 1 as if to **knit**, K2 tog, PSSO, do **not** cut yarn; with second yarn, slip 1 as if to **knit**, K2 tog, PSSO, cut yarn and draw end through st: one st.

Slip st onto crochet hook, ch 12; with **right** side facing, join with slip st to first st on second side; finish off.

general instructions

ABBREVIATIONS

ch	chain(s)
cm	centimeters
K	knit
M1	Make One
mm	millimeters
P	purl
PSSO	pass slipped stitch over
SSK	slip, slip, knit
st(s)	stitch(es)
tbl	through back loop(s)
tog	together
YO	yarn over

SYMBOLS & TERMS

★ — work instructions following ★ as many **more** times as indicated in addition to the first time.

( ) or [ ] — work enclosed instructions **as many** times as specified by the number immediately following or contains explanatory remarks.

colon (:) — the number(s) given after a colon at the end of a row or round denote(s) the number of stitches you should have on that row or round.

Yarn Weight Symbol & Names	LACE ⓪	SUPER FINE ①	FINE ②	LIGHT ③	MEDIUM ④	BULKY ⑤	SUPER BULKY ⑥
Type of Yarns in Category	Fingering, size 10 crochet thread	Sock, Fingering, Baby	Sport, Baby	DK, Light Worsted	Worsted, Afghan, Aran	Chunky, Craft, Rug	Bulky, Roving
Knit Gauge Range* in Stockinette St to 4" (10 cm)	33-40** sts	27-32 sts	23-26 sts	21-24 sts	16-20 sts	12-15 sts	6-11 sts
Advised Needle Size Range	000-1	1 to 3	3 to 5	5 to 7	7 to 9	9 to 11	11 and larger

*GUIDELINES ONLY: The chart above reflects the most commonly used gauges and needle sizes for specific yarn categories.

** Lace weight yarns are usually knitted on larger needles to create lacy openwork patterns. Accordingly, a gauge range is difficult to determine. Always follow the gauge stated in your pattern.

■□□□ BEGINNER	Projects for first-time knitters using basic knit and purl stitches. Minimal shaping.
■■□□ EASY	Projects using basic stitches, repetitive stitch patterns, simple color changes, and simple shaping and finishing.
■■■□ INTERMEDIATE	Projects with a variety of stitches, such as basic cables and lace, simple intarsia, double-pointed needles and knitting in the round needle techniques, mid-level shaping and finishing.
■■■■ EXPERIENCED	Projects using advanced techniques and stitches, such as short rows, fair isle, more intricate intarsia, cables, lace patterns, and numerous color changes.

GAUGE

The dishcloth dresses are written for medium weight 100% cotton yarn. Gauge is not of great importance; your dishcloth may be a little larger or smaller without changing the overall effect.

KNIT TERMINOLOGY	
UNITED STATES	INTERNATIONAL
gauge =	tension
bind off =	cast off
yarn over (YO) =	yarn forward (yfwd) **or**
	yarn around needle (yrn)

KNITTING NEEDLES		
UNITED STATES	ENGLISH U.K.	METRIC (mm)
0	13	2
1	12	2.25
2	11	2.75
3	10	3.25
4	9	3.5
5	8	3.75
6	7	4
7	6	4.5
8	5	5
9	4	5.5
10	3	6
10½	2	6.5
11	1	8
13	00	9
15	000	10
17	---	12.75
19	---	15
35	---	19
50	---	25

INCREASES
KNIT INCREASE

Knit the next stitch but do **not** slip the old stitch off the left needle *(Fig. 1a)*. Insert the right needle into the **back** loop of the **same** stitch and knit it *(Fig. 1b)*, then slip the old stitch off the left needle.

Fig. 1a

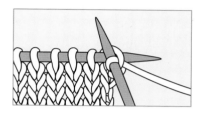

Fig. 1b

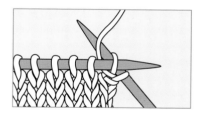

YARN OVER

Bring the yarn forward **between** the needles, then back **over** the top of the right needle, so that it is now in position to knit the next stitch *(Fig. 2)*.

Fig. 2

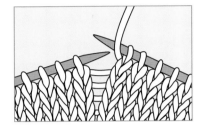

MAKE ONE *(abbreviated M1)*

Insert the **left** needle under the horizontal strand between the stitches from the **front** *(Fig. 3a)*. Then knit into the **back** of the strand *(Fig. 3b)*.

Fig. 3a

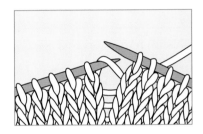

Fig. 3b

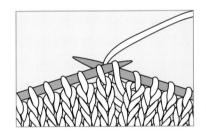

DECREASES
KNIT 2 TOGETHER
(abbreviated K2 tog)

Insert the right needle into the **front** of the first two stitches on the left needle as if to **knit** *(Fig. 4)*, then **knit** them together as if they were one stitch.

KNIT 2 TOGETHER THROUGH BACK LOOP
(abbreviated K2 tog tbl)

Insert the right needle into the **back** of the first two stitches on the left needle *(Fig. 6)*, then **knit** them together as if they were one stitch.

Fig. 4

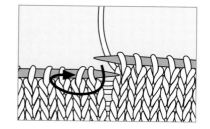

Fig. 6

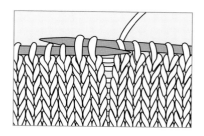

PURL 2 TOGETHER
(abbreviated P2 tog)

Insert the right needle into the **front** of the first two stitches on the left needle as if to **purl** *(Fig. 5)*, then **purl** them together as if they were one stitch.

Fig. 5

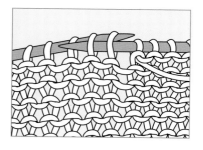

SLIP, SLIP, KNIT

(abbreviated SSK)

With yarn in back of work, separately slip two stitches as if to **knit** *(Fig. 7a)*. Insert the **left** needle into the **front** of both slipped stitches *(Fig. 7b)* and knit them together as if they were one stitch *(Fig. 7c)*.

SLIP 1, KNIT 1, PASS SLIPPED STITCH OVER

(abbreviated slip 1, K1, PSSO)

Slip one stitch as if to **knit** *(Fig. 8a)*. Knit the next stitch. With the left needle, bring the slipped stitch over the knit stitch *(Fig. 8b)* and off the needle.

Fig. 7a

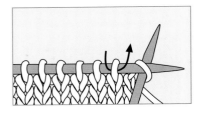

Fig. 8a

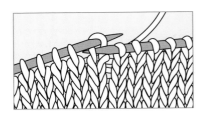

Fig. 7b

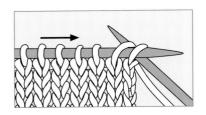

Fig. 8b

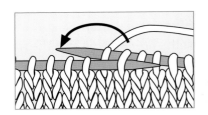

Fig. 7c

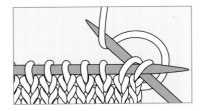

KNIT 3 TOGETHER

(abbreviated K3 tog)

Insert the right needle into the **front** of the first three stitches on the left needle as if to **knit** *(Fig. 9)*, then **knit** them together as if they were one stitch.

Fig. 9

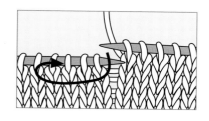

SLIP 1, KNIT 2 TOGETHER, PASS SLIPPED STITCH OVER

(abbreviated slip 1, K2 tog, PSSO)

Slip one stitch as if to **knit** *(Fig. 8a, page 44)*, then knit the next two stitches together *(Fig. 4, page 43)*. With the left needle, bring the slipped stitch over the stitch just made *(Fig. 10)* and off the needle.

Fig. 10

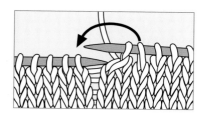

CHANGING COLORS
JOINING YARN AT THE BEGINNING OF A ROW

With the new color of yarn, leave a 6" (15 cm) end or tie a temporary knot around previous color yarn. The unused color of yarn can be carried up the side, twisting it every few rows. Cut the yarn when no longer needed, leaving a long end so that the ends can be woven in the back of the work.

JOINING YARN WITHIN A ROW

Wind the specified amount of yarn indicated in the instructions into a separate ball. Always keep the unused colors on the **wrong** side of the work. When changing colors, always pick up the new color yarn from **beneath** the dropped yarn and keep the color which has just been worked to the left *(Fig. 11)*. This will prevent holes in the finished piece. Take extra care to keep the tension even.

Fig. 11

BASIC CROCHET STITCHES

CHAIN *(abbreviated ch)*

With the stitch on crochet hook, ★ bring the yarn over the hook from **back** to **front**, catching the yarn with the hook and turning the hook slightly toward you to keep the yarn from slipping off, draw the yarn through the stitch *(Fig. 12)*; repeat from ★ for the required number of chains.

Fig. 12

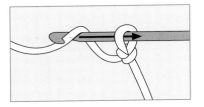

WORKING INTO A CHAIN

Insert the hook under the top two strands of each chain *(Fig. 13)*.

Fig. 13

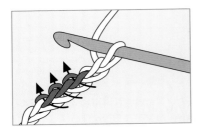

SLIP STITCH *(abbreviated slip st,*

Insert the hook in stitch indicated, bring the yarn over the hook and draw through stitch **and** through loop on hook (**slip st made,** *Fig. 14*).

Fig. 14

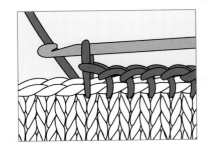

yarn information

The dishcloth dresses shown were made using
Lily® Sugar 'n Cream®, a 100% cotton Medium Weight Yarn.
Any Medium Weight Yarn may be used. It is best to refer to the
yardage/meters to determine how many balls or skeins to purchase.

For your convenience, listed below are the specific
colors used to create our photography models.

A NIGHT ON THE TOWN
Aqua - #01215 Robin's Egg Blue
Cream - #00003 Cream

PRINCESS FOR A DAY
#19209 Pastel Print

COMPANY'S COMING
Green - #00016 Dark Pine
Variegated - #20244 Green Twists

DRESS WITH APRON
Yellow - #00010 Yellow
Variegated - #02223 Mod Ombre

GOING DANCING #1
Blue - #01742 Hot Blue
Ecru - #01004 Soft Ecru

GOING DANCING #2
White - #00001 White
Aqua - #01215 Robin's Egg
Peach - #00042 Tea Rose
Yellow - #00010 Yellow

WEDDING DAY
#00001 White

HAPPY DAY #1
Cream - #00003 Cream
Aqua - #01215 Robin's Egg Blue
Peach - #00042 Tea Rose

HAPPY DAY #2
Variegated - #02220 Green Dream
Yellow - #00073 Sunshine

PROM DATE #1
Lavender - #00093 Soft Violet
Variegated - #00223 Violet Veil
Ombre

PROM DATE #2
Pink - #01444 Mod Pink
Variegated - #02445 Lava Lamp

GARDEN PARTY
#00046 Rose Pink

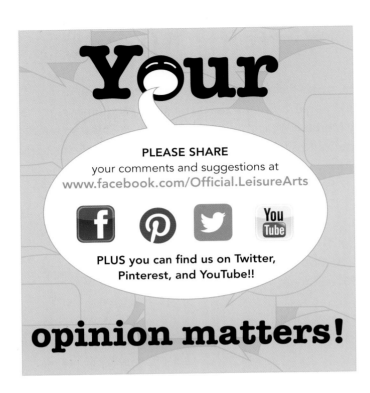

We have made every effort to ensure that these instructions are accurate and complete. We cannot, however, be responsible for human error, typographical mistakes, or variations in individual work.

Production Team: Technical Writer/Editor - Linda A. Daley; Editorial Writer - Susan Frantz Wile; Senior Graphic Artist - Lora Puls; Graphic Artist - Stacy Owens; Photo Stylists - Sondra Daniel and Lori Wenger; and Photographers - Jason Masters and Ken West.